ITI

A Bornean El

ITIN

A Bornean Elephant

**Jaswinder Kaur Kler, Benoit Goossens,
and Marc Ancrenaz**

Photography by
Rudi Delvaux

*For my sweet Rory,
The best hatier in the
whole Kinabatangan.
Love Benoit*

Natural History Publications (Borneo)
Kota Kinabalu

2014

Dedicated to the people who tirelessly work in the field to protect elephants and their habitats.

Published by

Natural History Publications (Borneo) Sdn. Bhd. (216807-X)
A913, 9th Floor, Wisma Merdeka Phase 1,
P.O. Box 15566,
88864 Kota Kinabalu, Sabah, Malaysia.
Tel: +6088-233098 Fax: +6088-240768
e-mail: info@nhpborneo.com
website: www.nhpborneo.com

in association with

Danau Girang Field Centre
C/o. Sabah Wildlife Department,
Wisma Muis, Block B, 5th Floor,
88100 Kota Kinabalu, Sabah, Malaysia.
Tel: +6088-341527 (Off.); +6012-8364005 (Mobile)
Fax: +6088-341528
e-mail: goossensbr@cardiff.ac.uk

HUTAN — Kinabatangan Orang-utan Conservation Programme
P.O. Box 17793,
88874 Kota Kinabalu, Sabah, Malaysia.
Tel: +6088-413293 (Off.); +6013-8756009 (Mobile)
Fax: +6088-413293
e-mail: ngo_hutan@yahoo.com

ITIN: A Bornean Elephant
by Jaswinder Kaur Kler, Benoit Goossens and Marc Ancrenaz
Photography by Rudi Delvaux

First published January 2014
ISBN 978-983-812-150-7

Half-title page: An elephant getting rid of parasites and cooling itself down by spraying soil on its back.
Frontispiece: A baby elephant learning to use its trunk under an elder's watchful eye.

Printed in Taiwan.

Contents

Fig. 1. This is Itin's story.

Introduction

I t is a misty and cool morning. Birds of many colours hop between leafless branches in the canopy and fly short distances to other trees, breaking the silence with a fusion of tunes. Across the river, women dressed in sarongs scrub laundry, squatting on wooden half-submerged floating platforms as their children take a quick dip before heading to school. Then the buzz of a boat engine interrupts the tranquil setting of an almost cloudless orange and purple sky at sunrise.

My name is Itin, and I am an eight-year-old male elephant. I live in a place called Kinabatangan, named after a mighty river that centuries ago drew traders from as far away as China, who wanted beeswax for candles, edible bird's nests, rattan vines and yes, elephant ivory. Today, seafarers no longer traverse up the river in traditional sailing vessels called junks, but the Kinabatangan in north-eastern Borneo continues to lure people from almost every corner of the world. Some are travellers who are attracted to this part of Malaysia for its iconic wildlife, birds and breathtaking scenery, a few carry out research so that the human race can learn to better manage the ecosystem and living things that depend on these landscapes. Indigenous people, mainly the Orang Sungai, literally translated as "river people", have for generations called the Kinabatangan their home, one that they are now forced to share with large agricultural estates after the decline of the timber boom in this region.

In faraway places where we do not exist in the wild, children draw us on sketching paper and colour us in pinks and blues, pasting their bedroom walls with pictures of happy elephants floating up into the sky, tugged by balloons. Tales of how mystical and intelligent we are get passed down through folklore in exotic lands, each story unique to the local area and passed down in languages foreign to our ears. People meet and suggest solutions to protect us, and some dedicate their lives to learning our ways, living alongside us

Fig. 2. A mother fitted with a satellite collar and her family foraging for food along the Kinabatangan River.

in forests and by the river bank. Tourists fly for many hours in the hope of seeing us in the wild, and school groups traverse up the river on nature interpretation programmes.

I have come to learn that this picture can change in an instant. I am on the alert as the speed-boat rumbles to a stop, splashing tiny waves on to the bank, just a few feet away from where I am foraging with my herd of 10, mainly female, relatives. I sense my mother's body stiffen, the way it does when her guard is up. Though I am young, I feel responsible for protecting her. We watch cautiously as a group of people walk slowly towards us. Millions love us, but many also label us a nuisance, a pest even. Hundreds, if not thousands, of my ancestors were killed here as pressing economic and development needs made their way into our natural forest habitat, most of which is no more, taken over by vast agricultural landscapes.

Only time will tell my fate. It is 2014 and this is my story.

Fig. 3. A Bornean elephant on a journey of discovery.

Origin

I t was an exceptionally warm day in the tropics, with a prolonged drought threatening to scorch a nearby peat swamp, when I learned from my mother and aunts about our roots. It was a long lesson, one that took several days, our elders taking turns to share their knowledge on why we now call the north-eastern part of Borneo our home.

There were several versions. My cousins and I hung on to every word, captivated by the stories that our elders were passing down to us.

An aunt was the first to speak. Just over a year before I was born there was excitement in the air. Word had quickly reached the

Fig. 4. Elephant families travel together in search of food and water.

Fig. 5. When young, elephants stick close to their mothers and other members of the family.

Kinabatangan floodplain that elephants in our part of the world were unique, that we were not the same as elephants on mainland Asia and Indonesia's Sumatra Island. I became curious when my aunt said DNA from dung samples sent all the way to a university in the United States showed elephants in Borneo were isolated more than 300,000 years ago from mainland Asia and Sumatra. My cousins and I learned from her that we were smaller in size than Asian elephants, and we had longer tails that reach the ground, larger ears and straight tusks. We were said to be a genetically distinct species, not descended from elephants brought by people via sea.

This discovery on the planet's third largest island made its way to the front pages of newspapers and was shared through emails, online news and television. It generated excitement in the world of conservation, and pride among locals. Apart from our physical features, we were described as a sub-species that is tamer, and mild tempered, and one that breeds at an earlier age.

When I was introduced to the world after 22 months in the warmth of my mother's belly, we had come to be known as the Borneo

Fig. 6. A baby looking for milk and protection from the sun under its mother's belly.

Fig. 7. Elephants are very curious animals and will group together when they face something unusual…

Fig. 8. Before moving away when their curiosity is satisfied.

Fig. 9. Borneo, the world's third largest island, is home to the Bornean elephant, which is smaller than the Asian elephant, but has a longer tail and larger ears.

Fig. 10. Itin investigating the wonders of Kinabatangan in Sabah.

Pygmy Elephant. Estimates place us at about 2000 individuals in the wild — perhaps fewer. Compared to surveys indicating 38,000 to 55,000 Asian elephants and half a million African elephants, the Bornean elephant, a lineage I am proud of, deserves and needs more attention.

After we digested this story and were done with asking questions, mother said we should play by the river before sunset, and to get some rest after that, as she wanted to tell us another version of our existence. We carefully stumbled down the bank and into the river to cool off, our banter focused on what we had just learned.

The next morning we gathered early and heard with curiosity that our origin in Borneo is not clear, despite science saying we are special to the island. Secretly, I was disappointed, but I did not show it. Mother took us on a journey dating back to the 18th century, when jungles were so thick that they arched tributaries. It was a time when the floodplain teemed with wildlife, and was home to indigenous people with tattoos on their bodies, their clothes made of tree bark, and their homes of bamboo and rattan.

She challenged us with the idea that we are from a lineage of imported elephants, that we were dispersed in time of trade and war. We looked at one another, confused. The first record she mentioned was that in 1750 the British East India Company presented a gift of elephants to the Sultan of Sulu, who ruled this region. The elephants were released on what is now Sabah's east coast. Another story, even older, and less known in local history, is that the Majapahit Empire based in Sumatra was a formidable force that extended to Brunei, also in Borneo, in the 12th century. As was the custom then, Majapahit sent a pair of elephants to areas they had conquered as a signal of their strength. This is how Brunei and Banjarmasin, regions located in Borneo, received two elephants each. This tradition may have then led to the birth of elephants on the island. At a cave in Brunei, a single fossil tooth was found, and over in Banjarmasin, a discovery of elephant bones was made in 1988. A molar is also said to have been found at the Niah Cave in the neighbouring Malaysian state of Sarawak. Glancing at her sister to get assurance on her story, my mother told us this could mean that we are of a lineage introduced to Borneo.

An older cousin spoke of another tale she had heard, that of tame Asian elephants from Thailand arriving in Sabah as late as the mid-1960s to aid the growth of the timber industry, which at that time relied heavily on our strength to pull logs. We vowed to keep these stories in our memories, and one day tell our children what we had so carefully listened to.

I know that there must be many more stories about our origin, and I hope more people will study our history and make discoveries about us.

Fig. 11. In Borneo, there are an estimated 2000 elephants, mostly in Sabah, but a few herds move back and forth between the Malaysian state and Kalimantan, Indonesia.

Legends

Modern-day stories place us at the centre of conflict with people, and growing loss of our home ranges. There are also stories that chronicle what people and governments are doing to safeguard our future, and we are increasingly the subject of heated debate. The same is the fate of our relatives in Africa, India and other parts of Asia.

In the past, barely half a century ago, we were heroes in local traditional stories, passed down orally from generation to generation. In the Kinabatangan, as in other places, folklore passed down among indigenous communities boasts of our intelligence, our ability to sense what is said about us, and how much we are respected. Today, these stories are hardly told, lost in the mists of tradition, eroded by fast-paced modernity, and safeguarded only by elders who can only hope their children and grandchildren will pass them on.

The first traditional story among the Orang Sungai is of a couple who ventured into the forest to collect roots and leaves needed to cure a villager who had fallen ill. This walk into the dense forest started at the crack of dawn, after receiving guidance through a dream on what was needed to prepare a traditional concoction for an illness. Unfortunately, the couple lost their way and, at sunset, decided to spend the night leaning against a giant tree. Hours later in the stillness of the night, they were awakened by a trumpeting sound. The couple were terrified, recognising the sound to be that of an elephant. In the past, villagers hardly ever saw elephants as jungles were still thick. At that time, my ancestors were not pushed to the edge of rivers, never needing to share space with people and agricultural estates, the way we are forced to now.

The couple relied on the legend that elephants were to be respected. In the local dialect, we are called Nenek (grandma), referring to our status as elders of the forest. The couple asked in silent prayer for Nenek to spare them, as they were only in the forest to gather supplies for a traditional concoction used in healing. They asked Nenek for guidance to lead them out as they were lost. At dawn, the couple saw a large male elephant in the distance, its ivory tusks reflecting tones of varying orange hues with the glow of the emerging sun. Unsure, and still afraid, they relaxed after a few moments when they saw the elephant flapping its ears and moving

its trunk up and down, gesturing at them. Taking this as a signal, they followed Nenek's trail, and were led to the river bank. In their hearts the grateful couple thanked Nenek, and related the story to villagers.

The second story is about a villager who needed a new boat so that he could catch fish and prawns in different parts of the river. With help from villagers, he felled a *merbau* tree, a tropical hardwood. After splitting the tree and carving out a boat, he realised that he was too deep in the jungle to pull the vessel to the river. Unsure of what to do, the man who desperately needed the boat recollected what his father had told him. He turned to Nenek for help. The villager made a plea — *"Nenek, please help me. I am poor, and I have no strength to pull this boat."* The man returned home and tried to think of ways to lower his boat into the river. Not long after, he saw the boat at the river bank behind his house. Deep in his heart he knew that Nenek had listened and helped in his time of need. The man pledged to always be respectful of elephants, telling his children, and those after them, to do the same.

There are many other legends that speak of our strength, helpful nature and grace. We have our own world, and we are always aware of what is happening around us. I know of elephants that have damaged homes, water tanks and vehicles. We trample on crops when we know of people who say bad things about us, or think of harming us. If we are in your way, it is only because there is very little left of our home. If I end up behind your kitchen, and you are afraid, ask me politely to move away, the way I often hear an old man whisper in the Sungai Idaan language *"Aki (Nenek), begedoh koi muyu sakotui. Memula kemi, bindokoi muyoh sokotueh."* (*"Nenek, please leave this place. We are afraid, please move to another space."*)

We were put on Earth alongside you and millions of other living things. We were created to help you in your hour of need, not to live in constant fear and dread of each other.

Fig. 12. (opposite). "The beast which passeth all others in wit and mind" — Greek philosopher Aristotle is known to have said about elephants.

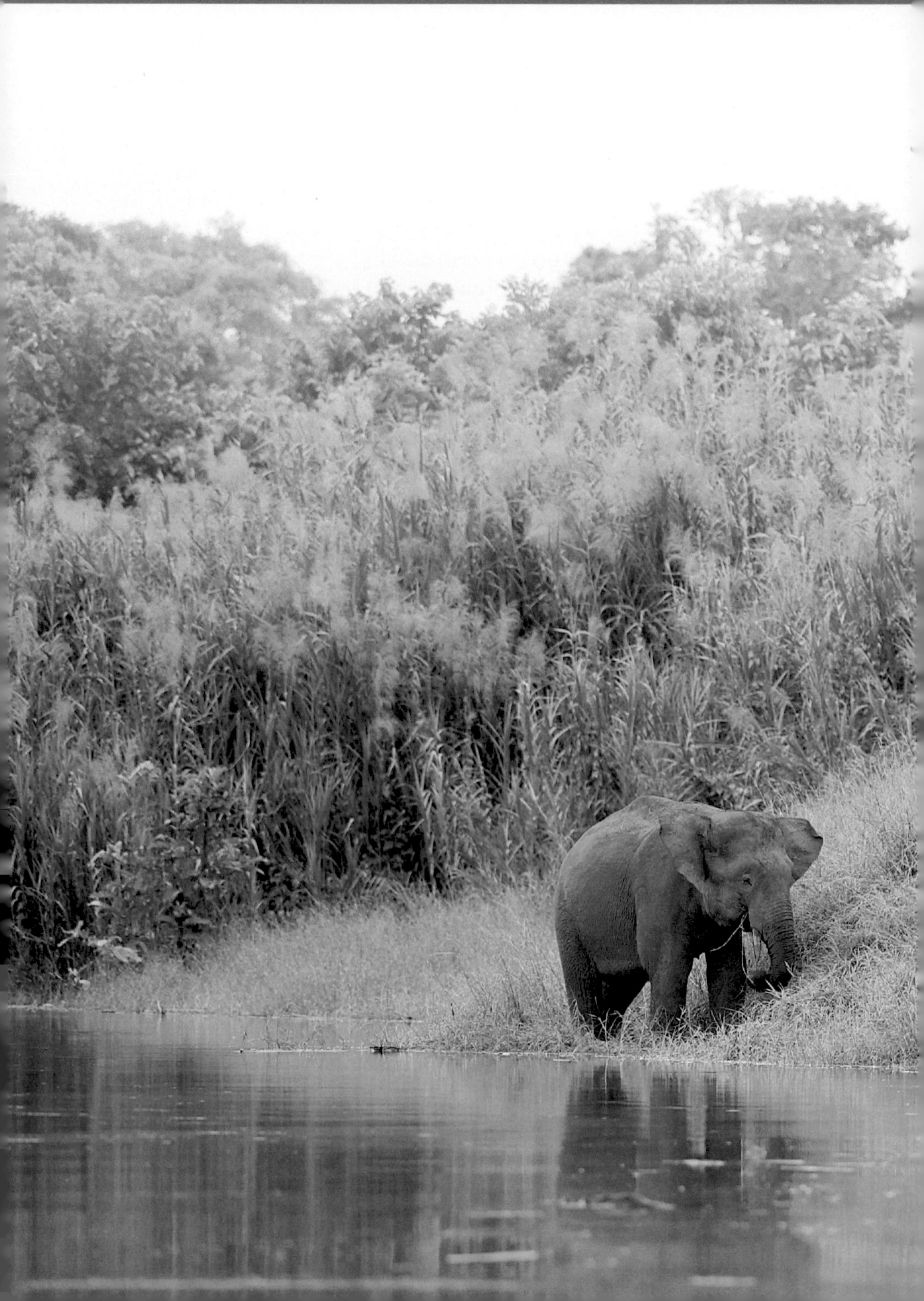

Our Home Range

Our ranging behaviour is strongly influenced by our need for water, minerals and certain types of food. From the time we are born we establish an area familiar to us, and this is known as our home range. This familiar area is determined by where the matriarch moves. Once a male leaves his group, he will find his own new home range. We stick to paths that we have used for years, and we can walk up to 10 kilometres in a day.

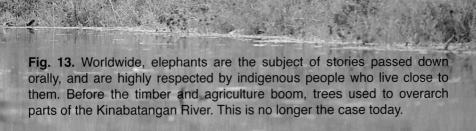

Fig. 13. Worldwide, elephants are the subject of stories passed down orally, and are highly respected by indigenous people who live close to them. Before the timber and agriculture boom, trees used to overarch parts of the Kinabatangan River. This is no longer the case today.

Fig. 14 (above). The Lower Kinabatangan Wildlife Sanctuary is largely made up of a floodplain ecosystem. **Fig. 15** (below). The 560-kilometre Kinabatangan River is the longest waterway in Sabah, and sustains one of the world's richest ecosystems.

Fig. 16 (above). The scenic Kinabatangan River by night has for centuries drawn people to its banks, as has many other parts of Borneo. **Fig. 17** (below). A tributary that supports elephants and other wildlife.

Fig. 19. A spiny vine.

Fig. 18. The lush canopy of the rainforest showing flowering trees. Sabah is a biodiversity hotspot, and its remaining rainforests are home to some of the most endangered wildlife on the planet, including the orang utan.

Fig. 20. A captivating sunset in Borneo.

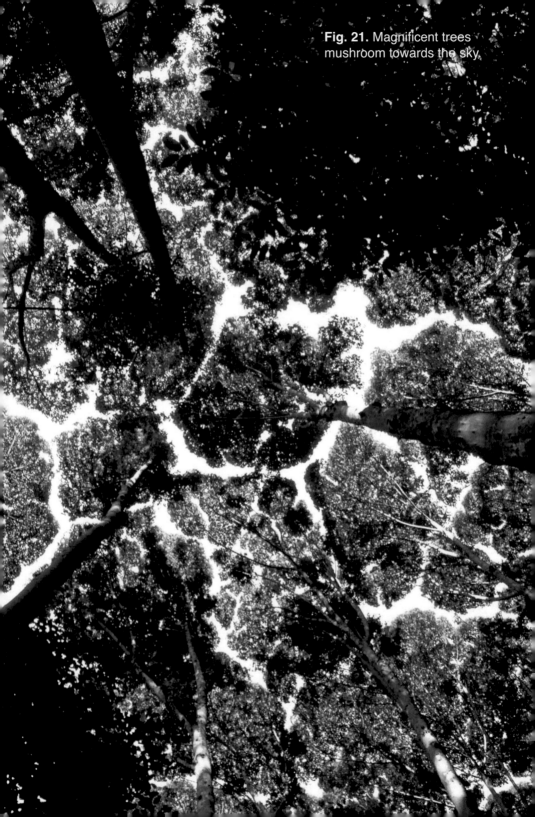

Fig. 21. Magnificent trees mushroom towards the sky.

Where We Live

Photos from almost a century ago show clear streams, forests that bend over into the waterway and thick vines that act as ladders for orang utan and other primates within this range. I wish I had been born at that time. All I see now are small pockets of forests, the landscape overtaken by agriculture, and a river that is the colour of the milky tea that people enjoy drinking at coffee shops all over Malaysia. Yet the little that is left of my home is peppered with swamp forests, oxbow lakes and limestone hills important for the survival of wildlife. We know how to travel in this landscape, but recently we have found ourselves feeling lost as we are forced to change our migration routes. A path we are familiar with today may no longer be passable just a year from now, and this leaves us in despair. I overheard my elders talking about a path that disappeared overnight when the forest was replaced with an oil palm plantation. My elders were children then, and had wept at dawn when they returned to a familiar forest, only to find it gone and fenced off. They had no choice but to turn back.

Borneo is a large island, but we live only in the south, east and centre of the Malaysian state of Sabah, and a few individuals, perhaps not more than 20, are in Indonesia's Kalimantan, very close to the border. No one in my family is sure why our population has not spread to other parts of Borneo. I did hear from one elder that maybe this is linked to the belief that my ancestors were brought only to the east coast of Borneo, and we did not have enough time to make our way to the entire island.

My herd and I are stuck in the Kinabatangan range, one of five locations elephants are found in Sabah. We may perhaps never meet elephants in the other four ranges as we are cut off from them by roads, plantations, villages and resorts. Sometimes I feel like we are walking in circles. There is not much left to forage on, forcing us to feed on oil palm shoots.

Fig. 23. Elephants have poor eyesight and depend on the scents like dung, urine and sweat to move about.

Our Unique Features

I know that you are curious about my trunk, so let me tell you what I use it for. With my trunk I tug at food and place meals into my mouth. This part of my body is made up of more than a thousand muscles, making it a very strong organ that can rip off entire branches. Sometimes we want food that is high up, so we coil our trunk around the tree and tug it until fruits drop. We also use it to drink by sucking in huge amounts of water, which we blow into our mouths. To keep parasites away and to ease discomfort from the sun's rays, I use my trunk to collect mud and soil, coiling it backwards, spraying this mixture on my back. When I bath, I depend on my trunk to hose water all over my back. I am sure you would have never guessed that I use it as a snorkel when I swim across rivers.

Fig. 24 (left). The trunk is used to gather food. **Fig. 25** (right). Collecting mud, later sprayed on the elephant's back to cool it down on a hot day.

Fig. 26 (left). The trunk is a strong organ, made up of over a thousand muscles. **Fig. 27** (above right). Elephants flap their ears constantly to regulate body temperature. When there is danger, they stiffen their ears and once they are assured there is no threat, they go back to flapping their ears. **Fig. 28** (below right). A rare sight of an elephant with a very short tail.

Just as people have their own ways of greeting one another, we entwine our trunks, similar to a handshake. Mothers and their young interact with one another in a playful way by using their trunks, and adults use it to caress one another during courtship. If we raise our trunks, it means that we are sending out a warning, or that we are aware of an impending threat. In times of danger we use our raised trunks to sniff, and our ears will expand and stiffen. If the threat is real, we can use our trunks to grasp intruders and fling them away. If there is no threat, we will lower our trunks and flap our ears.

Another interesting feature that we have is our ivory-coloured tusks, which are actually teeth. Unlike our cousins in Africa who all grow tusks, only male elephants in Asia have this feature. In females, very small tusks that may appear are known as tushes. Our tusks actually grow continuously at several centimetres a year, and we use them to dig for minerals like salt, and when we need to source water in areas away from rivers. This organ is living tissue and is not as strong or as solid as a rock although it looks like it is.

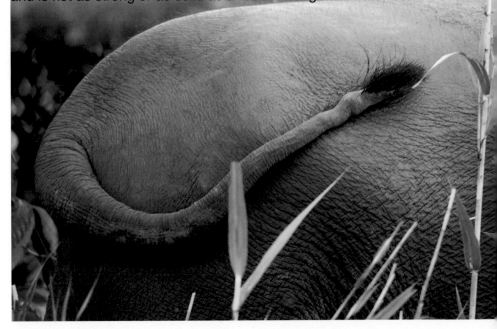

Fig. 29. If I am in your way, it is only because there is very little left of my home.

The more dominant tusk is shorter and rounder at its tip as it gets eroded with time. Just like trunks, our tusks have many uses; one of them is to mark trees to establish our territory. We use our tusks to poke trees to get pulp, and when we need to clear paths as we move about in our home ranges. To us, tusks are also weapons which we use if we feel threatened in any way. Sadly, as far back as the emergence of ancient civilisations in Europe, the Middle East and parts of Asia, elephants have always been prized for their tusks — used to make ivory carvings. Extensive literature points to China, Japan and India as centres for ivory carving, and the rise of the Babylonian and Persian civilisations across land routes between the west and India created trade for this commodity. The best ivory is said to have come from elephants in the Indian region of Orissa. Perhaps millions of elephants have died over many centuries, completely wiped out in some locations. In the 21st century there is no end to demand despite multi-agency crackdowns on poachers, smugglers, dealers and buyers.

Based on photographs and documentaries on television, most people think that we have no teeth. We have teeth that move horizontally, left to right, and right to left. As a new tooth grows at the back, the older and worn-out teeth fall out. Old elephants prefer softer food as they stop producing new teeth. When the last set of teeth fall, an elephant will die of starvation.

Fig. 30. We share this planet with you.

Our Social Behaviour

I am observing my family rest at midday, tired after having walked a long distance on our usual migration route. A baby lies close to her mother's belly, seeking comfort from her caregiver's warmth. My mother is sleeping in a standing position — her face resting on the bark of a tree that serves as a pillow, her legs crossed. The rest of us are lying down, our eyes closed, yet alert to sounds and movements. A broken branch falls to the ground nearby, waking us.

An older female cousin starts to talk, telling us that elephants form social groups. Compared to our friends in the animal kingdom,

Fig. 31. Elephants use their trunks to greet and bond.

Fig. 32. A mother coils her tail to a young elephant's trunk, leading it on a path.

Fig. 33. Young elephants are very social and spend a lot of time playing together. This will determine relationships between individuals once they become adults.

Fig. 34. Elephants regularly travel close to rivers and other water sources.

our social system is very complex. We have large brains that allow us to retain memories and shape behaviours. For a long time, people have observed elephants in the wild, and in Borneo we see interest among researchers who want to delve deeper into learning about us. These researchers — some from far away — follow us around, and take notes and photographs. I am sure that one day they will discover more of our secrets, and share them with the world.

Our intelligence and strong character are clear from day one — the day we are born. Within a few minutes, or at most a couple of hours after birth, we can stand up, but our movement is wobbly, and we squeak to get attention. Within three days we are able to walk close to our mother and follow her around. The first week is not without its challenges — we cannot see clearly and need our mothers to push us on with her trunk and front legs. We find our mothers through sound, touch and smell. Dealing with our trunk is the most difficult part — as a newborn, I remember tripping over it many times. But I was so happy when I turned a month old because I was finally able to use my trunk to pick up twigs, leaves and grass. During my fourth month I could pull out grass and leaves and eat these, and I was able to suck water into my trunk instead of directly drinking through the mouth. Until my sixth month I suckled as much as I did from the time I was born, as we need nutrition from both our mother and the surrounding vegetation to keep us healthy. I drank up to 11 litres of milk a day — that is about seven large mineral water bottles. On my first birthday I was able to eat on my own, and drink and groom myself. I continued to depend on milk from my mother for another year, and relied on her for protection as I learned the ropes of living. Up to the age of eight years we remain very near our mothers almost all the time.

Within our social system young elephants interact closely with other family members. Young ones seek comfort by rubbing their body against older ones, or by placing their trunk into the mouth of another elephant to find out what the other is eating. As a young child, whenever I placed my trunk into an adult's mouth I felt safe, calm and protected. It used to give me a lot of reassurance, this feeling that my family is around to safeguard me.

Calves and juveniles spend hours playing with older members of our group, opening a window for us to learn a variety of behaviours

Fig. 35. An adult coaxes a baby to move along after crossing a river.

that will help us as we grow older. If our mother is away looking for food, an aunt will take care of us. Scientists have termed this *allomothering*. If we need to, we will suckle on our relatives; this is known as *allosuckling*.

When I was a baby I loved to play with cousins of the same age. We enjoyed using our heads to push each other, and took great thrill in coiling our trunks to wrestle. Whenever I see my younger cousins chasing one another, climbing on each other, even in rivers, I recall this happy phase of my early days. The interesting thing about young elephants is that we males tend to be more playful, and we are not shy about reaching out to those from different groups. I made many friends as a very young child, and maybe one day I will see them again. My female cousins seem to prefer playing with babies, their motherly skills evident at a young age.

Now that I am older, I need to start learning the ropes of living an independent life. One day, my mother sat me down, and asked me to listen with an open heart. I was afraid and slightly upset when she told me that within a year I will have to leave the herd. She assured me that it is her duty to encourage me to leave, so that I can live a solitary life, the way males do. Now I understand why I have never seen my father. My mother comforted me, and told me that she will always hold me dear to her heart.

Fig. 36. Itin will soon leave his home, and will miss playtime with his family.

I asked her to tell me what to expect once I am on my own. I learned that day that juvenile males, around the ages of eight to nine years, leave the herd and their matriarch, and venture into unknown territory. Solitary juveniles then find an all-male group and become friends. This bachelor group learns to cooperate in searching for food, and we keep our strength and alert levels up by playing games. Our way of playing with one another is often mistaken as fighting. My mother told me that this is a skill that I need to survive in the harsh reality of a habitat that is shrinking by the day.

When I become an adult I will start to produce an oily substance that will appear on my forehead, and which will trickle down between my eyes. Scientists call this *musth* and claim that it is an indication that a male is ready to find a partner to mate with. This temporal gland secretion is accompanied by dribbling of urine, up to 350 litres daily, marking paths for potential mates. Males "advertise" themselves through a distinct vocalisation, and by producing a specific odour.

I was warned that in this situation, also known as immersion, I will behave aggressively to members of my group. Less time will be spent on eating to focus my energy on seeking a mate, requiring me to be in good health and to have strength to sustain the musth period, that can last up to four months. The downside of this period is the high levels of testosterone, associated with musth, that impact the immune system. I will have to expect to fall ill after the musth period is over as my body will become weak. It is starting to dawn on me that life is only going to get tough once I leave my family.

In contrast, the bond among females is extremely tight. A mother will pass all of her knowledge, including migration routes, to her daughter. If for any reason a young female is separated from her group, she is able to detect and identify spots that are familiar to her along her migration route. She will wait there until her group reappears to protect and nurture her.

A female elephant's love for her children and other young charges is a characteristic that stands out. I take comfort in the fact that the mother of my children will do the same, as I will not be around to see them grow up. One day, an aunt demonstrated this

Fig. 37. A matriarch trumpeting
as she gathers her family.

deep affection for her very young son. As we were walking along a muddy area my cousin was accidently trapped. His mother used her trunk to pull him out, with every ounce of strength in her body. Mothers protect their young when crossing rivers, always making sure that little ones make it safely across.

Let me share a story I was told by an aunt about this strong love and bond that adult females share with young ones. Crossing the Kinabatangan River, a family had almost made it across when suddenly a young elephant started wailing in pain at a muddy part of the river bank. An older female quickly returned to the juvenile, and saw that a crocodile was tugging at one of its legs. This brave elephant used the might of her weight to trample the reptile until it was forced to let go of the young elephant that was going to become its meal. The young elephant was injured, and had blood oozing from its leg but, with some coaxing and pushing by the older family member, made it safely up the bank.

Elephants have sensory skills and instincts that tell us we are related. I did not believe this until I came across two females trumpeting, using their trunks to form a physical bond. I came to learn that they were sisters who had been separated when their group had become too big.

Fig. 38. Playtime is a way of picking up much needed survival skills in a shrinking habitat.

How We Communicate

We have a well-developed communication system that sees us using multiple senses to listen, learn and to relate messages. Through our ears, eyes, taste buds and by touching, we can sense vibrations, prepare ourselves for possible attacks, and send out signals to other elephants. Although most of our communication is focused within our families, we do send out messages to other elephant groups, particularly when we need help.

Fig. 39. Greeting one another.

Fig. 40. Despite their size, elephants have a low-pitched sound that humans cannot hear.

Let me share with you what I know of African elephants. When members of a large group are separated by several kilometres — a deliberate move to minimise competition for food — they are able to send out acoustic signals that reach one another in case they need to regroup to face predators. In the African continent, elephant calves are at risk of being killed by lions and hyenas. Elephants protecting their young will growl at lions, and lions will roar back. The sounds that elephants make reach others despite huge distances, and soon, back-up arrives.

Some signals are meant for short-distance use, for an example if a baby falls into a river and the mother needs help from nearby groups. We also use vocal communication to keep our family together, and to locate lost members.

We use different frequencies to reach a range of distances. When we listen to sounds that come from other elephant groups, we are able to tell if the group is far away or nearby, just based on the type of signal they send.

The trumpet sound that we make is the most popular one known to you. We also use other sounds like roars, barks, snorts, growls and rumbles for both short- and long-distance communication.

In reality, we have a low-pitched sound that acts as our secret language — which you cannot hear, and one that our predators cannot capture. Scientists call this infrasound, and I know there are

Fig. 41. We are family.

people trying hard to learn and understand this secret language that elephants use.

Let me give you some examples of how we secretly speak to one another. The "greeting rumble" is used by adult females within the same family or group when they meet after a separation of several hours. A relatively soft, unmodulated sound accompanied by ear flapping is known as a "contact call" and is used when we are separated by up to a couple of kilometres during feeding. The "contact answer" is the response to the "contact call" and will become softer once we get closer. When a matriarch needs to get her group together before moving to a new location, she will use a soft rumble. A male in musth gives out a low-frequency sound known to scientists as the "motorcycle", several times within an hour. The low-frequency modulated "female chorus" is the response of several adult females to the musth rumble.

Few people know that we have poor eyesight, and we mostly view the world in a shade of grey. To stay safe, to find food and to carry on with our daily lives, chemical communication is very important to us. The smells of sweat, dung, urine and musth fluid send us a variety of signals. The smell of a mother's urine, for example, is known to an offspring from its very early days. If separated for over 20 years, a male elephant will know if his potential mate is actually his own mother just by the scent of her urine. This is one way we avoid inbreeding, a situation that could lead to the collapse of our population. Special hair, known as vibrissae, on the tip of our trunk also plays a sensory role, sending and exchanging chemical messages.

We have the best low-frequency hearing among mammals that have been tested. Some believe our hearing is better by between ten and a hundred times that of humans. If not for our shrinking habitat, you would find it difficult to see us as we know when people are around, and we prefer to stay away.

What We Eat

As a large mammal, we need lots of food to survive. In the Kinabatangan, researchers are continuing to find out the types of food that we eat so that better land use management practices can be put in place to protect our meal sources. They have identified over 130 plant species that our diet depends on, including long and short grasses and twigs from several different

Fig. 42. An elephant munching on long grass.

Figs. 43–46. Elephants eat up to four per cent of their body weight daily (above left); chewing oil palm leaves (above right); an elephant using its trunk to tug at leaves (below left); elephant dung (below right). **Fig. 47** (opposite). Apart from shrubs, elephants consume fruits, herbs, bark and aquatic plants.

types of shrubs. We are also fond of tree bark, roots, gingers, rattan, herbs and aquatic plants. During the fruiting season we look out for bananas, durians, and a local fruit known as *tarap*. We eat the equivalent of about four per cent of our body weight, which means that if I eventually weigh 3000 kilograms, I will need 120 kilograms of food each day.

Fig. 48. In the Kinabatangan, elephants depend on over 130 plant species.

Our Friends

I share my home with other wildlife, birds and insects. They come in many different colours, shapes and sizes. Some are very tiny, at least to me. Elephants are the largest land mammal, dwarfing most other warm-blooded animals that live in terrestrial ecosystems.

We each have our own ways of sending out calls — whistles, grunts, growls, chirps, roars, barks, hoots. As we make our way across patches of forests, swamps, rivers and other landscapes, our combined voices become the heartbeat of the Kinabatangan region. Many from the animal kingdom help regenerate the forest; by dispersing seeds, we ensure there are enough plants and fruits for our sustenance and for the needs of humans. We breathe life into the planet.

Fig. 49 (left). A male orang utan in the canopy. **Fig. 50** (right). A family of proboscis monkeys.

Fig. 51 (above left). Long-tailed macaque, one of the 10 species of primates in the Kinabatangan. **Fig. 52** (above right). Small-toothed palm civet is one of the numerous carnivore species present in the Kinabatangan. **Fig. 53** (below). Bearded pig.

Fig. 54. A Sunda clouded leopard sharing the same habitat.

Fig. 55 (above). A monitor lizard makes its way up the river bank. **Fig. 56** (below). A saltwater crocodile getting some warmth from the sun. **Fig. 57** (opposite). A rhinoceros hornbill picking up a fruit.

I respect the right that my friends have to find food and shelter. This was one of my earliest lessons in life. Although I have to remain vigilant when crossing rivers, or when resting at the bank of streams, the crocodile being a natural predator, I remain in awe of this reptile, which shares a long evolutionary history with elephants.

One of the most loved mammals here is the orang utan. Sometimes I spot one, always alone, the exception a mother with a young child. Older males are big and have padded cheeks, but have a sense of calmness about them as they pluck fruits and wild berries at the top of trees. I hardly see orang utan walking on the ground, and they never swim across streams as they do not like water. People have built them bridges made of ropes and fire hoses to link tributaries now that large trees with wide strong branches in the canopy that used to act as natural bridges have almost disappeared. Elusive by nature, maybe when no one is looking they cross these bridges. I am amazed at how graceful the orang utans are, and their ability to build new nests made of twigs and leaves on higher branches of trees each night. I wonder what it feels like to have a bed to sleep in.

This region has other primates, too. Playful pig-tailed and long-tailed macaques that swing through trees and balance themselves on bridges meant for the orang utan, their antics all the more pronounced when tourists excitedly take their photographs. Gibbons are also found here. Proboscis monkeys with large noses move in large family groups, and are especially active in the morning and before sunset, munching away on leaves, mainly in mangrove areas.

Birds fly freely here, and can see from above what our home actually looks like. Hornbills, kingfishers, storks and eagles perch on trees for a quick rest, and then continue to spread their wings in search of food. Small birds that live closer to the ground sometimes hop around, feeding on worms and almost microscopic insects on the forest floor. They flutter away when I get too close. Perhaps they are afraid I will trample them by accident with my large round feet.

The Sumatran rhinoceros, characterised by its single upward horn, is said to live here, but I have never seen one. They, too, are large and heavy, but not as big as us, and they eat similar types of food. Last week, a cousin told our family that time is running out for rhinos. I was shocked to learn that the best estimates are fewer than 10 individuals in Sabah. I start to feel anxious, and sad. I wonder about their desperate situation, and how much longer they will continue to exist. I start thinking about my fate.

Fig. 58. White-bellied sea eagles are common along the course of the river.

Our Home Today

For the past few days I have not slept well. I have kept to myself, in deep thought about what my cousin had told us. What if the clock starts to tick faster for Bornean elephants? Will we make it to the end of this century? I hang my head low, not in the mood to forage this morning.

My mother senses my fear, and comes close to me, using her trunk to caress my back. I tell her that I am very afraid about my future, and that of my children. She turns and gestures with her trunk for the rest of the family to gather.

As a mother, it is her duty to shield me from the truth so that I can enjoy my youth for as long as possible. But she feels that younger members of the family must know what is happening to our home.

My mother starts by telling us that along with two of her cousins, she has lived in this region for over 40 years. In her own words, and with deep sorrow tinged in her voice, this is her story:

Fig. 59. Oil palms shrouded in the morning mist.

Fig. 60 (above left). Land clearing, mainly for agricultural purposes. **Fig. 61.** (above right). Digging into soil to create a drain, further cutting wildlife access. **Fig. 62** (below). An area cleared for agriculture.

"My dear son Itin, and nephews and nieces, it is time for you to know what is happening to our home. Less than a century ago, during the time of my great-grandparents, we lived deep in the jungle. Along with other wildlife, we were free to roam and forage. The rich and diverse rainforest gave us plenty to eat and gurgling clear streams that rushed down from highlands in the interior provided us with water. My elders never had to venture too far."

"At that time, Borneo's jungles were dense and were teeming with wildlife. Borneo promised a sense of adventure and discovery, and soon, people from foreign lands started arriving on our shores. Some came to work here as administrators, others made their way to northern Borneo for trade reasons. There were hunters with guns, competing with indigenous people who used blowpipes to aim for deer, wild boar and other game. An American couple even came all the way to Borneo to film and photograph Borneo, the Kinabatangan River becoming their favourite spot. My elders never saw these activities as threats. Disturbances were small, constrained by labour that depended on the strength of man. There were no machines, there were very few vehicles. Communities who have lived here for centuries took only what they needed for shelter and food."

"The northern part of Borneo is large, and the forest was so thick that few dared to venture deep into it. There was a network of large trees, connected by protruding roots similar to veins, keeping the forest alive. My grandmother told me that she could hear sounds from within trees, and could feel soft vibrations from the ground. She reminded us all the time that trees are sacred, and must be respected. That they are alive and that they talk to one another. I can feel the energy of trees, and I hope that you can, too. But this energy is becoming weak."

"Young ones, today our home is not the same as it was when my elders were alive. Around the time I was born, the destruction started. My earliest memories are that of sounds once alien to us. Motorised machines screeched almost non-stop, felling trees that had taken hundreds of years to grow. In just a matter of minutes, we would hear trees crashing to the ground, birds and bees taking flight, wildlife scurrying away. The rumble of tractors and forklifts became a familiar sound as they ravaged the land, scarring our home."

"As you know by now, we have familiar routes that we use in our quest for food, water and minerals. I was about five years old, trailing a path we knew well, foraging along the way. We had not been on this slightly hilly route since the last rainy season a year before. We had decided to move to higher ground as the lower plains were flooded, and we were excited. The place we were headed to was among the best in terms of food variety and salt licks from which we gain minerals. Suddenly, our matriarch stopped in her tracks, and started trumpeting, sounding upset. From behind some tall trees we saw what looked like a clearing, and we edged our way forward, wanting to know what had triggered our leader to become distressed. That morning, my family and I wept."

"Ahead of us, for as far as we could see, lay a barren land, the yellowish brown soil exposed. There were remnants of tree stumps, and smoke escaped into the air, turning the blue sky grey. We spent

Fig. 63. Oil palms planted right up to the edge of the Kinabatangan River, while some other sections remain forested.

a long time, all of us lined up, just looking at what man had done. One of our best refuges was gone. Our food, our shelter, our salt licks — they were no more. There was silence all around us. The wildlife symphony was gone with the death of the forest. There was no sign of life. As we used our trunks to uncover the soil beneath our feet, just metres away from what was now a man-made edge of the forest, we discovered some of our friends whom we had met just a year ago. Some are slow-moving animals and could not flee on time. We formed a ring around them, staying on till nightfall as a sign of mourning."

"The next morning we retreated, using the same migratory path. We had less to eat as we had already foraged most of the same areas just weeks before. We reached a river, desperate for water. It had turned murky, but we had no choice but to drink from it. We had to be careful as huge numbers of logs were floating down, some at high speed. My mother had to pour water into my mouth as she did not want me to be hit by a log."

"That was the day my life became a struggle. We started to compete with man for space. Not a year would go by without my family losing yet another foraging area. Today we are squeezed into this region, unable to move along migratory paths, cut off by roads and plantations, unable to meet our families to form larger herds the way we used to. We have been separated from other herds for the last 25 years."

"We started getting into conflict with people. It was never our intention to trample on their crops, or to destroy their property and vehicles. Some of the only routes we had left were along rivers, which happen to be the best locations for villagers to settle as they depend on the river for food, water and transport. Soon there were complaints against us. One of my elders ate some crops and accidently damaged several tombstones as she made her way back to our family — and she was shot, left to die. We mourned for days. We started hearing of other families losing loved ones in brutal ways."

"My children, by the time you were born in the late 1990s and the early part of this millennium, the landscape had been transformed. The forest patches that we use now are pockets within large agricultural estates, similar to islands in the sea. The birds see this from above, we don't."

"There is better understanding now of our needs, and there is legislation to protect what is left of our home range. There are laws in place to jail people who kill elephants and other types of protected wildlife. But I must warn you to always keep your ears open. I feel sad to tell you that elephants are still shot by those who view us as pests. Yes, the number of elephants killed in recent years is small, but the anger against us is great. I say this because a few of the shot elephants were also butchered for no apparent reason, their parts left to decay. My son Itin, not too long ago when you were still a baby, the world was startled by the picture of an elephant head floating down the river. It had been decapitated, probably after it was shot."

It was dusk by the time my mother completed her story. I now understand why there are groups of people who follow us, and chase us away using cannons that make loud boom sounds. They use very bright lights to scare us away, and sometimes they scream at us. I find them annoying, but they are actually protecting us by guiding us out of plantations, farms and villages. They are selflessly serving our interests.

Fig. 64. A barge ferrying sand mined from the Kinabatangan River. Sand dredging is further eroding already narrow river banks that wildlife use as a pathway to move from one forested area to another.

Learning About Us

Unlike elephants that live in other parts of the world, very little is known about the Bornean sub-species. It is easier to study elephants that live in open spaces in vast areas like Africa and the Indian sub-continent. Here in Borneo, we prefer forests and it can be challenging for people to follow us around to record our behaviour and movement patterns.

In the past, some research was done, but in the last decade we have seen renewed interest in learning about us after our classification as a distinct sub-species. Our shrinking habitat and our plight for survival are the basis for studies that aim to find out what people can do better in order to co-exist with us.

One of the ways people study us is by hanging a collar around the neck of selected adults, usually the matriarch who holds the most knowledge. These collars use satellite technology to transmit messages on the location of families, allowing scientists to identify our movement patterns in different parts of Sabah. The findings of combined long-term studies are crucial to understanding what

Fig. 65. A researcher recording elephant movements and behaviour at the Kinabatangan River.

habitat fragmentation does to elephants. Those who study us find that our movement patterns have become irregular, that we sometimes spend weeks in one location, and then move very quickly to another area. Researchers are saying that our movements are random, but that it is clear we stay close to rivers and swamps as we need a lot of water. One long-term finding, published in a journal, sends a message of how we have had to shift our home ranges in search of food. Changes in land use have altered places we get food and where we find water and other resources.

Some study us through photos that are captured on cameras triggered by our movements. They know when we move through a certain area, and who we are with. If we happen to stop close to a camera, they study our behaviour. There are also people who pick up our dried dung to study what sort of food we eat, and how much of a certain fruit or plant we consume. Some combine their research with direct observations, sitting in makeshift huts. I recognise some of them, but yet, just to be cautious, we threaten to charge at them. Man should never get too comfortable with us. A bull in musth may, for no apparent reason, attack a person.

Fig. 66 (left). Tracing elephants through their footsteps. **Fig. 67** (right). Measuring the tail of an elephant during collaring operations.

Current and Future Threats

A month has passed since my mother spoke about our fragmented home. Today I experienced the perils of a habitat that is not large enough for us all. We heard a cry for help and soon we found a female elephant, about my age, in pain. The foot of her right foreleg was caught in a snare, and together we pulled her away from the trap. The rope snare, close to a plantation, was meant for a wild boar or deer, set by someone living nearby. She continued to scream in pain, and someone who saw what had happened informed the authority in charge of wildlife conservation. The next morning, several people came and removed the snare, treating her wound. My aunt whispered to us that the trapped elephant was fortunate that help had come quickly. Other elephants, and even sun bears and clouded leopards, have died from infections that spread from wounds. The hairs on my back stood up when she said one in ten elephants in the Kinabatangan and the rest of our ranges have scars of snares around their legs.

Fig. 68. A herd forced to walk through an oil palm estate in a fragmented landscape.

Fig. 69. Decades ago, it was difficult to spot elephants as they moved about in a dense forest. Today, the gentle giant sometimes finds itself walking on logging and plantation roads.

After we left, my aunt sat us down to tell us about threats that we face today, and what might happen in the future. I was not sure if I could stomach more bad news, but I listened carefully as she started to speak:

"Our biggest threat today is the loss of our natural habitat. The forest is fragmented, and we are slowly becoming more and more isolated from other herds. Although there is a decline in converting forests for agriculture, the threat remains real as not all jungles are fully protected. Some jungle patches are on privately owned land that belongs to plantation companies or individuals. They can at any time clear the forest to plant the commercially lucrative crop, oil palm. Time and again we find our paths blocked by these plantations, and their electric fences. What did we do wrong? Why was our path taken away? Why is our natural home now a sea of oil palm?"

"This shrinking habitat is leading to more conflicts. Sometimes we enter oil palm estates from points where there are no electric fences, just to get to another patch of forest. Although we do not like the taste, we eat some palm fruits and young shoots because we have no choice. We have to eat so that we will have energy to move. Some plantation owners get angry at us, and threaten us. To plantation owners we are a nuisance that costs them money in damaged crops and fences. But I know that some are trying very hard to create paths for us so that we can continue to move within the fragmented Kinabatangan region, and in other home ranges."

"Paths along the river are getting tighter, and in some places we are completely cut off by oil palms that reach the edge of the water. We walk for hours, only to find our paths blocked, yet again. We were here first, and my plea is for planters to replant forest trees close to rivers. It is becoming more congested here in the Kinabatangan."

"In forest reserves our movements are hampered by logging. No, not all forest reserves are fully protected. Some allow for harvesting of timber on a sustainable basis, which means that a work plan and maps are drawn up on areas to be logged and zones that will be rehabilitated. Some zones, such as watersheds, are not disturbed. Humans often forget that we need a large area, and the cycle pattern of logging in forest reserves impacts us when our migratory routes are disturbed."

"Another threat we face comes from tourism. We understand that people want to see us in the wild, but with this comes a price — riverside lodges to accommodate travellers. In their planning, people sometimes do not understand that they are blocking our path by constructing buildings and jetties. It is ironic that the very reason a tourist visits our home may cause us and other wildlife to be pushed into further distress, and into harm's way. We also notice more and more tourists coming close to us on river banks, getting out of boats. We do not like this, and ask for people to respect our already limited space. What I am truly afraid of is that one day one of us might attack someone out of the need to protect our family. Some of us are starting to feel stressed. We constantly worry about where our next meal will come from, or if we will end up seeing another blocked path. Sometimes we are even aggressive to those who study us. I do not wish for us to be labelled a danger to people, giving them a reason to kill us. It is people who are a threat to us."

At this point, my aunt stops talking. She is overcome with sadness, and turns away to regain her composure. My mother offers to continue telling us of threats that we face.

"My son, Itin, and children of this family, this is my message to you. I am growing old, but you have a long way to go, and will need to find a way to live with humans. I am worried if you will be able to. Please stay calm as I tell you this. I heard from another family that there are plans to build a road for people to travel on and for crop produce to be sent from estates to mills. This road will cut through an important conservation area, which is currently difficult for hunters and poachers to access. We, and other wildlife, will face further risks. I hope what I have heard is not true."

"Another threat that we face comes from far beyond our home. The ivory trade is thriving, demand forever increasing for this prized possession. Although our home is outside the traditional ivory trade routes of Africa and India, greed and love for money can drive people to the furthest of places to source ivory. Recent dead elephants here in Sabah were found with their tusks missing — could this be a sign of poaching? Were these elephants killed on the pretext of getting

Fig. 70. This elephant's right foreleg was trapped in a snare, leading to serious injury and was rescued by the Sabah Wildlife Department.

rid of pests? Finished ivory products were recently found on sale in a city in Sabah. A couple of years ago, a pair of elephant tusks were found in the possession of a Malaysian citizen as this person entered a nearby Bornean town across the international border. I wonder if they came from one of us."

"Poisoning of our water or food — either deliberately or by accident — is a threat, too. In other parts of the world, elephants have been known to collapse and die for no reason after eating or drinking. I am overcome with sadness in telling you that several elephants in a different home range not too far from ours were recently found dead. They are believed to have met death due to toxic poisoning."

"It is becoming more difficult for herds to meet since the forest has mostly been replaced with oil palms. We are at risk of not being able to find mates from beyond our family circle. If our genes are of the same stock we will end up giving birth to babies that are weak, and who may not be able to endure the stresses of a changed landscape."

As my mother ends her part of the story, all of us are in tears. We huddle close to one another, locked in embrace till late into the night.

Fig. 71. Tourists fly from all over the world to get a glimpse of Bornean elephants in the wild. As important as the sector is for the local economy, tour operators and travellers must respect the space that elephants need.

What We Need

I speak on behalf of all elephants in Borneo. We have sent enough distress signals and it is time for action. Waiting it out, hoping that a solution will fall into place will just make the situation worse for my family, and all elephants in Borneo.

First, stop clearing whatever forest patches are left, especially in the Kinabatangan region. Do not convert any more land for agriculture. Contrary to what some think, or falsely believe, we cannot survive on just eating one type of plant.

Next, give up part of your land, especially at river banks, and make a commitment to replant fast-growing forest trees and fruit trees, and nurture young saplings until they are strong enough to withstand periods of drought and flooding. Create corridors to re-establish a network of continuous forests so that we will have access to more areas for foraging. These corridors must be wide enough for our families to pass through. Real commitment is needed for this, not just lip service. It is time for you to return what rightfully belongs to us and other wildlife. From what we now know, we expect conflicts to arise between us and humans in the very near future if nothing is done to reverse current ways of using land.

We also do not like to be forcibly moved from one place to another. People call this translocation, and often it is done with good intentions but we cannot speak to protest. Sadly, sometimes elephants are moved to get rid of "difficult" elephants. Another worry I have is the management of our population through culling. Although I do not see this happening in future because of the legal protection we are now given, it was done in the past and could be reintroduced. Let me tell you of an example from Africa. Adults were culled, and babies were sent to "orphanages" or rehabilitation centres. When these elephants became adults, they killed rhinos and people. For a while, humans could not understand why this was happening. Finally it dawned on them that when elephants are removed from their family unit and placed in a group of peers, they stop behaving the way they should. Translocation and culling are issues that people who manage us need to think about.

Borneo is a hotspot for nature-based tourism. Elephants are the stars of tour packages, and are prominently displayed in advertisements. We do not mind tourism that educates travellers about how vulnerable we are. Unfortunately, the focus today seems to be more on promising tourists that they will see us and other animals — forgetting that we are wildlife and can choose to not be visible. Instead, we find visitors coming closer to us, encroaching on our habitat, and disturbing us as we rest.

We hope that people will continue to study us, and highlight dangers that we face. Those who have the authority to make decisions must listen to what scientists are proposing now, and what they may suggest in the future.

Is There Hope?

Yet another month has whizzed by, and it is business as usual in the Kinabatangan. We found another blocked path this morning. Just before sunset, I left my family to get a feel of what it will be like when I am ready to venture out on my own. I walked into a snare hidden under some dried leaves. My left foreleg is trapped. I am alone and in pain.

Will you help me?

Fig. 72 (opposite). There are growing conflicts between humans and elephants, as indicated by evidence of uprooted oil palms. **Fig. 73** (above). "Wake up, Mother…."

Fig. 74. A high price to pay for development: old growth forest makes way for an oil palm plantation.

Acknowledgements

The authors thank Mr Abdul Karim Abdul Hamid, Ms Nurzhafarina Othman, Mr Sulaiman Ismail and the late Mr P.S. Shim for their valuable input in the research process. A special thank you goes to the Elephant Family for funding support in the writing of this book.

We wish to acknowledge the Kinabatangan Orangutan Conservation Programme (KOCP) Elephant Conservation Unit, the Sukau Honorary Wildlife Wardens team, the Wildlife Rescue Unit, the River Keeper Unit, the KOCP field research assistants, Ms Nurzhafarina Othman and Mr Jibius Dausip for their hard work on the ground. We thank the Sabah Wildlife and Sabah Forestry Departments for supporting elephant conservation work in Sabah.

The Danau Girang Field Centre and HUTAN-KOCP thank the following sponsors for their support on elephant research and conservation in Sabah: Abraham Shared Earth Foundation, Arcus Foundation, Association of Zoos and Aquariums, Elephant Family, Fondation Ensemble, Mohamed bin Zayed Species Conservation Fund, Sea World and Busch Gardens Conservation Fund, Shining Hope Foundation, Stichting Bring the Elephant Home, The Asian Elephant Foundation, US Fish and Wildlife Service's Asian Elephant Conservation Fund, Wildlife Conservation Network, Wood Tiger Foundation, Women's Work Foundation, World Land Trust, zoos of Apenheul, Basel, Beauval, Chester, Cincinnati, Cleveland, Columbus, Hogle, Houston, la Palmyre, Oregon, Philadelphia, Phoenix, Saint Louis, Toronto, Victoria and Woodland Park.

Photo credits:

HUTAN: Fig. 1; Fig. 7–8; Fig. 10; Fig. 12; Fig. 18 (1st half of page); Fig. 21; Fig. 37; Fig. 63; Fig. 64; Fig. 69; Fig. 70.
Sabah Wildlife Department: Fig. 73.

Further Reading

Alfred, R., Ahmad, A.H., Payne, J., Williams, C., Ambu, L.N., How, P.M., Goossens, B. (2012). Home range and ranging behaviour of Bornean elephant (*Elephas maximus borneensis*) females. *PLoS ONE* 7(2): e31400.

Alter, S. (2004). *Elephas maximus: A Portrait of the Indian Elephant*. Houghton Mifflin Harcourt. 336 pages.

Cranbrook, E., Payne, J., Leh, C.M.U. (2008). Origin of the elephants *Elephas maximus* of Borneo. *Sarawak Museum Journal* 63: 1–25.

deSilva, G.S. (1968). Elephants of Sabah. *Sabah Society Journal* 3: 169–181.

Estes, J.G., Othman, N., Ismail, S., Ancrenaz, M., Goossens, B., Ambu, L.N., Estes, A.B., Palmiotto, P.A. (2012). Quantity and configuration of available elephant habitat and related conservation concerns in the Lower Kinabatangan Floodplain of Sabah, Malaysia. *PLoS ONE* 7(10): e44601.

Fernando, P., Vidya, T.N.C., Payne, J., Stuewe, M., Davison, G., Alfred, R.J., Andau, P., Bosi, E., Kilbourn, A., Melnick, D.J. (2003). DNA analysis indicates that Asian elephants are native to Borneo and are therefore a high priority for conservation. *PLoS Biology* 1(1): e6.

Sabah Wildlife Department (2011). *Elephant Action Plan 2012–2016*. Kota Kinabalu, Sabah, Malaysia. 30 pages.

Sukumar, R. (1993). *The Asian Elephant: Ecology and Management*. Cambridge Studies in Applied Ecology and Resource Management. Cambridge University Press. 272 pages.

Sukumar, R. (1996). *Elephant Days and Nights: Ten Years with the Indian Elephant*. Oxford University Press, USA. 224 pages.

Sukumar, R. (2003). *The Living Elephants: Evolutionary Ecology, Behaviour, and Conservation*. Oxford University Press, USA. 496 pages.

Useful Links

www.facebook.com/Kinabatangan (HUTAN-Kinabatangan Orangutan Conservation Project).

www.facebook.com/pages/Danau-Girang-Field-Centre (Danau Girang Field Centre).

www.hutan.org.my (NGO HUTAN).

www.cardiff.ac.uk/biosi/facilities/danaugirangfieldcentre/index.html (Danau Girang Field Centre).

www.wwf.org.my (WWF-Malaysia).

www.elephantfamily.org (Elephant Family).

www.wildlife.sabah.gov.my (Sabah Wildlife Department).

Index